To:

From:

Message:

Published by Christian Art Publishers
PO Box 1599, Vereeniging, 1930, RSA

© 2024
First edition 2024

Designed by Christian Art Publishers

Cover designed by Christian Art Publishers
Images used under license from Shutterstock.com

Printed in China

ISBN 978-0-638-00166-2

24 25 26 27 28 29 30 31 32 33 – 10 9 8 7 6 5 4 3 2 1

PROMISES
FROM
The Word
— FOR MEN —

CHRISTIAN ART
PUBLISHERS

Contents

Abilities

"Rise up; this matter is in
your hands. We will support you,
so take courage and do it."

Ezra 10:4 NIV

For God gave us a spirit not of fear
but of power and love and self-control.

2 Timothy 1:7 ESV

Work willingly at whatever you do,
as though you were working for the
Lord rather than for people.

Colossians 3:23 NLT

"This is the word of the Lord
to Zerubbabel: Not by might,
nor by power, but by My Spirit,
says the Lord of hosts."

Zechariah 4:6 ESV

Accomplishments

For who makes you different
from anyone else? What do you
have that you did not receive?
And if you did receive it, why do
you boast as though you did not?
1 Corinthians 4:7 NIV

Two are better than one, because they
have a good reward for their labor.
Ecclesiastes 4:9 NKJV

Through God we will do valiantly,
for it is He who shall tread
down our enemies.
Psalm 60:12 NKJV

The end of the matter;
all has been heard. Fear God
and keep His commandments,
for this is the whole duty of man.
Ecclesiastes 12:13 ESV

Advice

The way of a fool is right in his own
eyes, but a wise man listens to advice.
Proverbs 12:15 ESV

Get all the advice and instruction you can,
so you will be wise the rest of your life.
Proverbs 19:20 NLT

For lack of guidance a nation falls,
but victory is won through many advisers.
Proverbs 11:14 NIV

Timely advice is lovely,
like golden apples in a silver basket.
Proverbs 25:11 NLT

"I will instruct you and teach you
in the way you should go;
I will guide you with My eye."
Psalm 32:8 NKJV

Ambition

Make it your ambition to lead
a quiet life: You should mind your own
business and work with your hands,
just as we told you, so that your
daily life may win the respect of
outsiders and so that you will not
be dependent on anybody.

1 Thessalonians 4:11-12 NIV

"For what profit is it to a man
if he gains the whole world,
and is himself destroyed or lost?"

Luke 9:25 NKJV

It has always been my ambition
to preach the gospel where Christ
was not known, so that I would not be
building on someone else's foundation.

Romans 15:20 NIV

Anger

"In your anger do not sin": Do not let
the sun go down while you are still angry.
Ephesians 4:26 NIV

He who is slow to wrath
has great understanding, but he
who is impulsive exalts folly.
Proverbs 14:29 NKJV

Stop being angry! Turn from your rage!
Do not lose your temper—
it only leads to harm.
Psalm 37:8 NLT

Know this, my beloved brothers: let every
person be quick to hear, slow to speak,
slow to anger; for the anger of man does
not produce the righteousness of God.
James 1:19-20 ESV

Attitude

You must have the same attitude that
Christ Jesus had. Though He was God,
He did not think of equality with
God as something to cling to.
Instead, He gave up His divine privileges;
He took the humble position of a slave
and was born as a human being.

Philippians 2:5-7 NLT

And whatever you do in word or deed,
do all in the name of the Lord Jesus, giving
thanks to God the Father through Him.

Colossians 3:17 NKJV

Do not be conformed to this world,
but be transformed by the renewal
of your mind, that by testing you may
discern what is the will of God,
what is good and acceptable and perfect.

Romans 12:2 ESV

Bitterness

Let all bitterness, wrath, anger,
clamor, and evil speaking be
put away from you, with all malice.
Ephesians 4:31 NKJV

Hatred stirs up conflict,
but love covers over all wrongs.
Proverbs 10:12 NIV

See to it that no one fails to obtain
the grace of God; that no "root of
bitterness" springs up and causes trouble,
and by it many become defiled.
Hebrews 12:15 ESV

Now, however, it is time to forgive
and comfort him. Otherwise he may
be overcome by discouragement.
2 Corinthians 2:7 NLT

Blameless

He will also keep you firm to the end,
so that you will be blameless on
the day of our Lord Jesus Christ.

1 Corinthians 1:8 NIV

Do all things without complaining
and disputing, that you may become
blameless and harmless, children of God
without fault in the midst of a crooked
and perverse generation, among whom
you shine as lights in the world.

Philippians 2:14-15 NKJV

I appeal to you therefore, brothers,
by the mercies of God, to present
your bodies as a living sacrifice,
holy and acceptable to God,
which is your spiritual worship.

Romans 12:1 ESV

Brokenness

"See, LORD, how distressed I am!
I am in torment within, and in
my heart I am disturbed, for I have been
most rebellious. Outside, the sword
bereaves; inside, there is only death."
Lamentations 1:20 NIV

The sacrifices of God are a broken
spirit, a broken and a contrite heart—
these, O God, You will not despise.
Psalm 51:17 NKJV

O God, listen to my cry! Hear my prayer!
From the ends of the earth, I cry to You
for help when my heart is overwhelmed.
Lead me to the towering rock of safety.
Psalm 61:1-2 NLT

The LORD is near to the brokenhearted
and saves the crushed in spirit.
Psalm 34:18 ESV

Burnout

Save me, O God! For the waters have
come up to my neck. I sink in
deep mire, where there is no foothold;
I have come into deep waters,
and the flood sweeps over me.

Psalm 69:1-2 ESV

This is what the Sovereign Lord,
the Holy One of Israel, says:
"In repentance and rest is your salvation,
in quietness and trust is your strength."

Isaiah 30:15 NIV

"He gives power to the faint,
and to him who has no might He
increases strength. Even youths shall
faint and be weary, and young men
shall fall exhausted; but they who wait
for the Lord shall renew their strength."

Isaiah 40:29-31 ESV

Business

Go to the ant, you sluggard!
Consider her ways and be wise,
which, having no captain, overseer
or ruler, provides her supplies
in the summer, and gathers
her food in the harvest.
Proverbs 6:6-8 NKJV

A false balance is an abomination to
the LORD, but a just weight is His delight.
Proverbs 11:1 ESV

Do you see any truly competent
workers? They will serve kings rather
than working for ordinary people.
Proverbs 22:29 NLT

He who tills his land will have
plenty of bread, but he who follows
frivolity will have poverty enough!
Proverbs 28:19 NKJV

Call of God

But you are a chosen people,
a royal priesthood, a holy nation,
God's special possession, that you may
declare the praises of Him who called you
out of darkness into His wonderful light.

1 Peter 2:9 NIV

For God saved us and called us to live
a holy life. He did this, not because we
deserved it, but because that was His plan
from before the beginning of time—
to show us His grace through Christ Jesus.

2 Timothy 1:9 NLT

Do not repay evil for evil or reviling
for reviling, but on the contrary,
bless, for to this you were called,
that you may obtain a blessing.

1 Peter 3:9 ESV

Character

Blessed is the man who walks not in
the counsel of the ungodly, nor stands
in the path of sinners, nor sits in the
seat of the scornful; but his delight
is in the law of the LORD, and in
His law he meditates day and night.
Psalm 1:1-2 NKJV

"Obedience is better than sacrifice,
and submission is better than
offering the fat of rams."
1 Samuel 15:22 NLT

Even a child makes himself
known by his acts, by whether
his conduct is pure and upright.
Proverbs 20:11 ESV

"Blessed are the pure in heart,
for they shall see God."
Matthew 5:8 NKJV

Children

Children are a heritage from the LORD,
offspring a reward from Him.
Like arrows in the hands of a warrior
are children born in one's youth.
Blessed is the man whose
quiver is full of them.
Psalm 127:3-5 NIV

Fathers, do not provoke your children
to anger, but bring them up in the
discipline and instruction of the Lord.
Ephesians 6:4 ESV

Train up a child in the way he
should go, and when he is old
he will not depart from it.
Proverbs 22:6 NKJV

Grandchildren are the crown of the aged,
and the glory of children is their fathers.
Proverbs 17:6 ESV

Christlikeness

And He said to all, "If anyone would
come after Me, let him deny himself
and take up his cross daily and follow Me."
Luke 9:23 ESV

"You must be compassionate,
just as your Father is compassionate."
Luke 6:36 NLT

For to this you have been called,
because Christ also suffered for you,
leaving you an example, so that you
might follow in His steps. He committed
no sin, neither was deceit found in
His mouth. When He was reviled,
He did not revile in return;
when He suffered, He did not
threaten, but continued entrusting
Himself to Him who judges justly.
1 Peter 2:21-23 ESV

Church

Let us not neglect our meeting together,
as some people do, but encourage
one another, especially now that the
day of his return is drawing near.
Hebrews 10:25 NIV

And they devoted themselves to
the apostles' teaching and the fellowship,
to the breaking of bread and the prayers.
And awe came upon every soul, and many
wonders and signs were being done through
the apostles. And all who believed were
together and had all things in common.
Acts 2:42-44 ESV

So we, being many, are one body
in Christ, and individually
members of one another.
Romans 12:5 NKJV

Commitment

"And whoever does not bear his cross
and come after Me cannot be My disciple.
For which of you, intending to build a
tower, does not sit down first and count the
cost, whether he has enough to finish it…"
Luke 14:27-28 NKJV

Commit your way to the LORD; trust in
Him and He will do this: He will make
your righteous reward shine like the dawn,
your vindication like the noonday sun.
Psalm 37:5-6 NIV

Brothers, I do not consider that I have
made it my own. But one thing I do:
forgetting what lies behind and straining
forward to what lies ahead, I press on
toward the goal for the prize of the
upward call of God in Christ Jesus.
Philippians 3:13-14 ESV

Communication

Do not let any unwholesome talk come out
of your mouths, but only what is helpful
for building others up according to their
needs, that it may benefit those who listen.
Ephesians 4:29 NIV

Let your speech always be gracious,
seasoned with salt, so that you may know
how you ought to answer each person.
Colossians 4:6 ESV

There is one who speaks like
the piercings of a sword, but the
tongue of the wise promotes health.
Proverbs 12:18 NKJV

May these words of my mouth and
this meditation of my heart
be pleasing in Your sight, LORD,
my Rock and my Redeemer.
Psalm 19:14 NIV

Compassion

When He went ashore He saw a great
crowd, and He had compassion on
them, because they were like sheep
without a shepherd. And He began
to teach them many things.

Mark 6:34 ESV

Praise be to the God and Father of
our Lord Jesus Christ, the Father
of compassion and the God of all comfort,
who comforts us in all our troubles,
so that we can comfort those in
any trouble with the comfort we
ourselves receive from God.

2 Corinthians 1:3-4 NIV

The LORD is compassionate
and gracious, slow to anger,
abounding in love.

Psalm 103:8 NIV

Compromise

Daniel resolved not to defile himself
with the royal food and wine, and he
asked the chief official for permission
not to defile himself this way.

Daniel 1:8 NIV

Let not sin therefore reign in your
mortal body, to make you obey its passions.

Romans 6:12 ESV

Beloved, do not imitate what is evil,
but what is good. He who does
good is of God, but he who
does evil has not seen God.

3 John 1:11 NKJV

"Seek the Kingdom of God
above all else, and live righteously,
and He will give you everything you need."

Matthew 6:33 NLT

Confession

But I confess my sins; I am
deeply sorry for what I have done.
Psalm 38:18 NLT

I said, "Lord, be merciful to me;
heal my soul, for I have sinned against You."
Psalm 41:4 NKJV

Confess your sins to one another
and pray for one another, that you may
be healed. The prayer of a righteous
person has great power as it is working.
James 5:16 ESV

If we confess our sins, He is faithful
and just and will forgive us our sins
and purify us from all unrighteousness.
1 John 1:9 NIV

Conflict

For in my inner being I delight in
God's law; but I see another law at work
in me, waging war against the law of
my mind and making me a prisoner
of the law of sin at work within me.

Romans 7:22-23 NIV

A servant of the Lord must not
quarrel but must be kind to everyone,
be able to teach, and be patient
with difficult people.

2 Timothy 2:24 NLT

"You have heard that it was said,
'An eye for an eye and a tooth for a tooth.'
But I say to you, Do not resist the one
who is evil. But if anyone slaps you on the
right cheek, turn to him the other also."

Matthew 5:38-39 ESV

Consequences

The tongue can bring death or life;
those who love to talk will
reap the consequences.
Proverbs 18:21 NLT

Do not be deceived, God is
not mocked; for whatever
a man sows, that he will also reap.
Galatians 6:7 NKJV

But if you do wrong, be afraid, for he does
not bear the sword in vain. For he is the
servant of God, an avenger who carries
out God's wrath on the wrongdoer.
Romans 13:4 ESV

No discipline seems pleasant at the time,
but painful. Later on, however, it produces
a harvest of righteousness and peace for
those who have been trained by it.
Hebrews 12:11 NIV

Contentment

For the sake of Christ, then,
I am content with weaknesses,
insults, hardships, persecutions,
and calamities. For when
I am weak, then I am strong.
2 Corinthians 12:10 ESV

But godliness with contentment is
great gain. For we brought nothing
into the world, and we can take
nothing out of it. But if we have food
and clothing, we will be content with that.
1 Timothy 6:6-8 NIV

Let your conduct be without covetousness;
be content with such things as you have.
For He Himself has said, "I will
never leave you nor forsake you."
Hebrews 13:5 NKJV

Courage

Strengthen the weak hands,
and make firm the feeble knees.
Isaiah 35:3 ESV

"Be strong and courageous!
Do not be afraid or discouraged.
For the LORD your God is
with you wherever you go."
Joshua 1:9 NLT

Be of good courage, and He shall strengthen
your heart, all you who hope in the LORD.
Psalm 31:24 NKJV

"Having hope will give you courage.
You will be protected and will rest in safety."
Job 11:18 NLT

Be watchful, stand firm in the faith,
act like men, be strong.
1 Corinthians 16:13 ESV

Crisis

Yea, though I walk through the valley
of the shadow of death, I will fear no evil;
for You are with me; Your rod
and Your staff, they comfort me.
Psalm 23:4 NKJV

For He will conceal me there when
troubles come; He will hide me
in His sanctuary. He will place me
out of reach on a high rock.
Psalm 27:5 NLT

God is our refuge and strength,
an ever-present help in trouble.
Therefore we will not fear,
though the earth give way and the
mountains fall into the heart of the sea,
though its waters roar and foam and
the mountains quake with their surging.
Psalm 46:1-3 NIV

Cross

And being found in appearance
as a man, He humbled Himself and
became obedient to the point of death,
even the death of the cross.
Philippians 2:8 NKJV

He canceled the record of the
charges against us and took it
away by nailing it to the cross.
Colossians 2:14 NLT

…and through Him God reconciled
everything to Himself. He made peace
with everything in heaven and on earth
by means of Christ's blood on the cross.
Colossians 1:20 NLT

By this we know love, that He laid
down His life for us, and we ought to
lay down our lives for the brothers.
1 John 3:16 ESV

Death

For the trumpet will sound,
the dead will be raised imperishable,
and we will be changed.
1 Corinthians 15:52 NIV

Since you have been raised to
new life with Christ, set your sights
on the realities of heaven…
Think about the things of heaven…
Colossians 3:1-2 NLT

For we who are in this tent groan,
being burdened, not because we want to
be unclothed, but further clothed,
that mortality may be swallowed up by life.
2 Corinthians 5:4 NKJV

For to me, to live is
Christ and to die is gain.
Philippians 1:21 NIV

Deceit

You shall destroy those who speak
falsehood; the Lord abhors the
bloodthirsty and deceitful man.
Psalm 5:6 NKJV

No one who practices deceit shall
dwell in my house; no one who utters
lies shall continue before my eyes.
Psalm 101:7 ESV

A false witness will not go unpunished,
and whoever pours out lies will not go free.
Proverbs 19:5 NIV

Yes, what joy for those whose record
the Lord has cleared of guilt,
whose lives are lived in complete honesty!
Psalm 32:2 NLT

Debt

The rich rules over the poor,
and the borrower is the slave of the lender.
Proverbs 22:7 ESV

Let no debt remain outstanding,
except the continuing debt to love
one another, for whoever
loves others has fulfilled the law.
Romans 13:8 NIV

Pay to all what is owed to them: taxes to
whom taxes are owed, revenue to whom
revenue is owed, respect to whom respect
is owed, honor to whom honor is owed.
Romans 13:7 ESV

But if anyone does not provide for
his own, and especially for those of
his household, he has denied the faith
and is worse than an unbeliever.
1 Timothy 5:8 NKJV

Decision-Making

"…choose this day whom you
will serve, whether the gods your fathers
served in the region beyond the River,
or the gods of the Amorites in whose
land you dwell. But as for me and
my house, we will serve the LORD."
Joshua 24:15 ESV

Trust in the LORD with all your heart
and lean not on your own understanding;
in all your ways submit to Him,
and He will make your paths straight.
Proverbs 3:5-6 NIV

Teach me Your way, O LORD;
I will walk in Your truth;
unite my heart to fear Your name.
Psalm 86:11 NKJV

Depression

From the depths of despair, O LORD,
I call for Your help. Hear my cry,
O Lord. Pay attention to my prayer.
Psalm 130:1-2 NLT

I waited patiently for the LORD; He turned
to me and heard my cry. He lifted me out
of the slimy pit, out of the mud and mire;
He set my feet on a rock and gave me a
firm place to stand. He put a new song in
my mouth, a hymn of praise to our God.
Psalm 40:1-3 NIV

The righteous cry out, and the LORD
hears them; He delivers them from
all their troubles. The LORD is close
to the brokenhearted and saves
those who are crushed in spirit.
Psalm 34:17-18 NIV

Diligence

Be diligent to present yourself
approved to God, a worker who
does not need to be ashamed,
rightly dividing the word of truth.
2 Timothy 2:15 NKJV

The soul of the sluggard craves
and gets nothing, while the soul
of the diligent is richly supplied.
Proverbs 13:4 ESV

The hand of the diligent will rule,
but the lazy man will be put to forced labor.
Proverbs 12:24 NKJV

Therefore, beloved, looking forward to
these things, be diligent to be found by
Him in peace, without spot and blameless.
2 Peter 3:14 NKJV

Disappointment

I will lift up my eyes to the hills—
from whence comes my help?
My help comes from the LORD,
who made heaven and earth.

Psalm 121:1-2 NKJV

Do not let your heart envy sinners,
but always be zealous for the fear of
the LORD. There is surely a future hope
for you, and your hope will not be cut off.

Proverbs 23:17-18 NIV

"God is not man, that He should lie,
or a son of man, that He should
change His mind. Has He said,
and will He not do it? Or has He
spoken, and will He not fulfill it?"

Numbers 23:19 ESV

Discipline

"Think about it: Just as a parent
disciplines a child, the LORD your God
disciplines you for your own good."
Deuteronomy 8:5 NLT

My son, do not despise the LORD's
discipline or be weary of His reproof,
for the LORD reproves him whom He loves,
as a father the son in whom he delights.
Proverbs 3:11-12 ESV

No discipline seems pleasant at the time,
but painful. Later on, however, it produces
a harvest of righteousness and peace
for those who have been trained by it.
Hebrews 12:11 NIV

Whoever loves instruction loves knowledge,
but he who hates correction is stupid.
Proverbs 12:1 NKJV

Discretion

I, wisdom, dwell with prudence,
and I find knowledge and discretion.
Proverbs 8:12 ESV

Be sober-minded; be watchful.
Your adversary the devil prowls
around like a roaring lion,
seeking someone to devour.
1 Peter 5:8 ESV

When I was a child, I spoke and thought
and reasoned as a child. But when
I grew up, I put away childish things.
1 Corinthians 13:11 NLT

The discretion of a man makes
him slow to anger, and his glory
is to overlook a transgression.
Proverbs 19:11 NKJV

Effectiveness

Likewise, my brothers, you also have died
to the law through the body of Christ,
so that you may belong to another,
to Him who has been raised from the dead,
in order that we may bear fruit for God.

Romans 7:4 ESV

"I am the vine, you are the branches.
He who abides in Me, and I in him,
bears much fruit; for without
Me you can do nothing."

John 15:5 NKJV

By faith these people overthrew kingdoms,
ruled with justice, and received what God
had promised them…Their weakness was
turned to strength. They became strong
in battle and put whole armies to flight.

Hebrews 11:33-34 NLT

Employers

"Do not make your hired workers wait
until the next day to receive their pay."
Leviticus 19:13 NLT

"You shall not oppress a hired worker who
is poor and needy...You shall give him
his wages on the same day, before the sun
sets (for he is poor and counts on it)."
Deuteronomy 24:14-15 ESV

Masters, give your bondservants
what is just and fair, knowing that
you also have a Master in heaven.
Colossians 4:1 NKJV

Now to the one who works, his wages
are not counted as a gift but as his due.
Romans 4:4 ESV

Employees

No accounting of this money was
required from the construction
supervisors, because they were
honest and trustworthy men.
2 Kings 12:15 NLT

Trustworthy messengers refresh
like snow in summer. They revive
the spirit of their employer.
Proverbs 25:13 NLT

Lazy people irritate their employers,
like vinegar to the teeth
or smoke in the eyes.
Proverbs 10:26 NLT

If your boss is angry at you,
don't quit! A quiet spirit can
overcome even great mistakes.
Ecclesiastes 10:4 NLT

Enthusiasm

Let the heavens rejoice, and let the
earth be glad; and let them say among
the nations, "The Lord reigns."
1 Chronicles 16:31 NKJV

You have turned my mourning into joyful
dancing. You have taken away my clothes
of mourning and clothed me with joy.
Psalm 30:11 NLT

Clap your hands, all peoples!
Shout to God with loud songs of joy!
Psalm 47:1 ESV

Blessed are the people who know
the joyful sound! They walk, O Lord,
in the light of Your countenance.
Psalm 89:15 NKJV

Excuses

"But they all alike began to make excuses…
Then the master of the house
became angry and said to his servant,
'Go out quickly to the streets and lanes
of the city, and bring in the poor
and crippled and blind and lame…'
For I tell you, none of those men who
were invited shall taste my banquet.'"
Luke 14:18, 21, 24 ESV

"If I had not come and spoken
to them, they would have no sin,
but now they have no excuse for their sin."
John 15:22 NKJV

The lazy person claims,
"There's a lion on the road!
Yes, I'm sure there's a lion out there!"
Proverbs 26:13 NLT

Failure

If we confess our sins, He is faithful
and just and will forgive us our sins and
purify us from all unrighteousness.
1 John 1:9 NIV

For a righteous man may fall
seven times and rise again, but the
wicked shall fall by calamity.
Proverbs 24:16 NKJV

My flesh and my heart may fail,
but God is the strength of my
heart and my portion forever.
Psalm 73:26 ESV

He who covers his sins will not
prosper, but whoever confesses and
forsakes them will have mercy.
Proverbs 28:13 NKJV

Faith

Now faith is the assurance
of things hoped for,
the conviction of things not seen.
Hebrews 11:1 ESV

He replied, "If you have faith as small
as a mustard seed, you can say to this
mulberry tree, 'Be uprooted and planted
in the sea,' and it will obey you."
Luke 17:6 NIV

Without faith it is impossible to please
Him, for he who comes to God must
believe that He is, and that He is a rewarder
of those who diligently seek Him.
Hebrews 11:6 NKJV

So faith comes from hearing, that is,
hearing the Good News about Christ.
Romans 10:17 NLT

Faithfulness

A faithful person will be richly
blessed, but one eager to get rich
will not go unpunished.
Proverbs 28:20 NIV

"I will not remove from him
My steadfast love or be false
to My faithfulness."
Psalm 89:33 ESV

"The LORD, the LORD, the compassionate
and gracious God, slow to anger,
abounding in love and faithfulness."
Exodus 34:6 NIV

Let us hold fast the confession
of our hope without wavering,
for He who promised is faithful.
Hebrews 10:23 ESV

Fear

God is our refuge and strength,
an ever-present help in trouble.
Therefore we will not fear, though
the earth give way and the mountains
fall into the heart of the sea.

Psalm 46:1-2 NIV

"Behold, God is my salvation,
I will trust and not be afraid;
'For YAH, the LORD,
is my strength and song;
He also has become my salvation.'"

Isaiah 12:2 NKJV

"Don't be afraid, for I am with you.
Don't be discouraged, for I am
your God. I will strengthen you
and help you. I will hold you up
with My victorious right hand."

Isaiah 41:10 NLT

Finishing

It is better not to make a vow
than to make one and not fulfill it.
Ecclesiastes 5:5 NIV

Finishing is better than starting.
Patience is better than pride.
Ecclesiastes 7:8 NLT

And I am sure of this, that He who
began a good work in you will bring it to
completion at the day of Jesus Christ.
Philippians 1:6 ESV

"However, I consider my life worth
nothing to me; my only aim is to finish
the race and complete the task the Lord
Jesus has given me—the task of testifying
to the good news of God's grace."
Acts 20:24 NIV

Focus

My heart is fixed, O God, my heart
is fixed: I will sing and give praise.
Psalm 57:7 KJV

I press on toward the goal for the prize of
the upward call of God in Christ Jesus.
Philippians 3:14 ESV

"Be strong and very courageous. Be careful
to obey all the instructions Moses gave
you. Do not deviate from them, turning
either to the right or to the left. Then you
will be successful in everything you do."
Joshua 1:7 NLT

Jesus replied, "No one who puts a hand
to the plow and looks back is fit for
service in the kingdom of God."
Luke 9:62 NIV

Forgiveness

"If My people who are called by My name will humble themselves, and pray and seek My face, and turn from their wicked ways, then I will hear from heaven, and will forgive their sin and heal their land."

2 Chronicles 7:14 NKJV

"Though your sins are like scarlet, they shall be as white as snow; though they are red as crimson, they shall be like wool."

Isaiah 1:18 NIV

"My wayward children," says the LORD, "come back to Me, and I will heal your wayward hearts."

Jeremiah 3:22 NLT

If we confess our sins, He is faithful and just to forgive us our sins and to cleanse us from all unrighteousness.

1 John 1:9 NKJV

Fellowship

And they devoted themselves to the
apostles' teaching and the fellowship,
to the breaking of bread and the prayers.
Acts 2:42 ESV

But if we are living in the light, as God
is in the light, then we have fellowship
with each other, and the blood of Jesus,
His Son, cleanses us from all sin.
1 John 1:7 NLT

"For where two or three gather in
My name, there am I with them."
Matthew 18:20 NIV

Therefore encourage one another
and build each other up,
just as in fact you are doing.
1 Thessalonians 5:11 NIV

Generosity

One person gives freely,
yet gains even more; another withholds
unduly, but comes to poverty.
A generous person will prosper;
whoever refreshes others will be refreshed.
Proverbs 11:24-25 NIV

Whoever is generous to the poor
lends to the Lord, and He will
repay him for his deed.
Proverbs 19:17 ESV

Whoever sows sparingly will also reap
sparingly, and whoever sows bountifully
will also reap bountifully. Each one
must give as he has decided in his heart,
not reluctantly or under compulsion,
for God loves a cheerful giver.
2 Corinthians 9:6-7 ESV

Goals

Let love be your highest goal!
1 Corinthians 14:1 NLT

Therefore let us pursue the things
which make for peace and the things
by which one may edify another.
Romans 14:19 NKJV

Let your eyes look straight ahead;
fix your gaze directly before you.
Give careful thought to the paths
for your feet and be steadfast in all
your ways. Do not turn to the right
or the left; keep your foot from evil.
Proverbs 4:25-27 NIV

Do you not know that in a race all the
runners run, but only one receives the
prize? So run that you may obtain it.
1 Corinthians 9:24 ESV

God's Will

The LORD will fulfill His purpose
for me; Your steadfast love,
O LORD, endures forever. Do not
forsake the work of Your hands.
Psalm 138:8 ESV

"I will instruct you and teach you
in the way you should go;
I will guide you with My eye."
Psalm 32:8 NKJV

"He has told you, O man, what is good;
and what does the LORD require of you
but to do justice, and to love kindness,
and to walk humbly with your God?"
Micah 6:8 ESV

Rejoice always, pray continually,
give thanks in all circumstances; for this
is God's will for you in Christ Jesus.
1 Thessalonians 5:16-18 NIV

Gossip

A dishonest man spreads strife,
and a whisperer separates close friends.
Proverbs 16:28 ESV

Do not speak evil of one another, brethren.
He who speaks evil of a brother and judges
his brother, speaks evil of the law and
judges the law. But if you judge the law,
you are not a doer of the law but a judge.
James 4:11 NKJV

Fire goes out without wood,
and quarrels disappear when gossip stops.
Proverbs 26:20 NLT

Let no corrupting talk come out of
your mouths, but only such as is good
for building up, as fits the occasion, that
it may give grace to those who hear.
Ephesians 4:29 ESV

Gratitude

Enter His gates with thanksgiving;
go into His courts with praise. Give
thanks to Him and praise His name.
Psalm 100:4 NLT

Do not be anxious about anything, but in
every situation, by prayer and petition, with
thanksgiving, present your requests to God.
Philippians 4:6 NIV

In everything give thanks; for this is the
will of God in Christ Jesus for you.
1 Thessalonians 5:18 NKJV

Give thanks to the LORD, for He is good,
for His steadfast love endures forever.
Psalm 136:1 ESV

This is the day the LORD has made.
We will rejoice and be glad in it.
Psalm 118:24 NLT

Greed

"Watch out! Be on your guard against all kinds of greed; life does not consist in an abundance of possessions."
Luke 12:15 NIV

A greedy man stirs up strife, but the one who trusts in the LORD will be enriched.
Proverbs 28:25 ESV

Don't love money; be satisfied with what you have. For God has said, "I will never fail you. I will never abandon you."
Hebrews 13:5 NLT

Those who desire to be rich fall into temptation and a snare, and into many foolish and harmful lusts which drown men in destruction and perdition.
1 Timothy 6:9 NKJV

Health

He heals the brokenhearted
and binds up their wounds.
Psalm 147:3 NIV

My son, pay attention to what I say;
turn your ear to my words. Do not let
them out of your sight, keep them within
your heart; for they are life to those who
find them and health to one's whole body.
Proverbs 4:20-22 NIV

A merry heart does good, like medicine,
but a broken spirit dries the bones.
Proverbs 17:22 NKJV

"Physical training is good, but training
for godliness is much better, promising
benefits in this life and in the life to come."
1 Timothy 4:8 NLT

Helper

"He is your shield and helper
and your glorious sword."
Deuteronomy 33:29 NIV

The Lord is my strength and my shield;
my heart trusted in Him, and I am
helped; therefore my heart greatly rejoices,
and with my song I will praise Him.
Psalm 28:7 NKJV

So we say with confidence, "The Lord
is my helper; I will not be afraid.
What can mere mortals do to me?"
Hebrews 13:6 NIV

"But the Helper, the Holy Spirit,
whom the Father will send in My name,
He will teach you all things
and bring to your remembrance
all that I have said to you."
John 14:26 ESV

Holiness

"Holy, holy, holy is the LORD of hosts;
the whole earth is full of His glory!"
Isaiah 6:3 NKJV

May He strengthen your hearts so that
you will be blameless and holy in the
presence of our God and Father when our
Lord Jesus comes with all His holy ones.
1 Thessalonians 3:13 NIV

"Consider them holy, because I the LORD
am holy—I who make you holy."
Leviticus 21:8 NIV

Do you not know that you are the temple
of God and that the Spirit of God dwells
in you? If anyone defiles the temple of God,
God will destroy him. For the temple
of God is holy, which temple you are.
1 Corinthians 3:16-17 NKJV

Hope

And so, Lord, where do I put my
hope? My only hope is in You.
Psalm 39:7 NLT

Let us hold fast the confession of
our hope without wavering, for
He who promised is faithful.
Hebrews 10:23 NKJV

Through Christ you have come to trust
in God. And you have placed your faith
and hope in God because He raised Christ
from the dead and gave Him great glory.
1 Peter 1:21 NLT

And hope does not put us to shame,
because God's love has been poured out
into our hearts through the Holy Spirit,
who has been given to us.
Romans 5:5 NIV

Humility

Clothe yourselves, all of you,
with humility toward one another,
for "God opposes the proud but gives
grace to the humble." Humble yourselves,
therefore, under the mighty hand of God so
that at the proper time He may exalt you.
1 Peter 5:5-6 ESV

By humility and the fear of the LORD
are riches and honor and life.
Proverbs 22:4 NKJV

Humble yourselves before the Lord,
and He will lift you up.
James 4:10 NIV

Before destruction a man's heart is haughty,
but humility comes before honor.
Proverbs 18:12 ESV

Hypocrisy

"What right have you to recite My statutes or take My covenant on your lips? For you hate discipline, and you cast My words behind you."
Psalm 50:16-17 ESV

If one turns away his ear from hearing the law, even his prayer is an abomination.
Proverbs 28:9 ESV

"I hate all your show and pretense— the hypocrisy of your religious festivals and solemn assemblies."
Amos 5:21 NLT

"Hypocrite! First remove the plank from your own eye, and then you will see clearly to remove the speck from your brother's eye."
Matthew 7:5 NKJV

Intimacy

Marriage should be honored by all,
and the marriage bed kept pure,
for God will judge the adulterer
and all the sexually immoral.
Hebrews 13:4 NIV

Flee from sexual immorality.
Every other sin a person commits
is outside the body, but the sexually
immoral person sins against his own body.
1 Corinthians 6:18 ESV

"Didn't the LORD make you one with
your wife? In body and spirit you are His.
And what does He want? Godly children
from your union. So guard your heart;
remain loyal to the wife of your youth."
Malachi 2:15 NLT

Jealousy

"You shall not covet your
neighbor's house; you shall not
covet your neighbor's wife, nor his
male servant, nor his female servant,
nor his ox, nor his donkey,
nor anything that is your neighbor's."
Exodus 20:17 NKJV

For where jealousy and selfish
ambition exist, there will be
disorder and every vile practice.
James 3:16 ESV

Anger is cruel and fury overwhelming,
but who can stand before jealousy?
Proverbs 27:4 NIV

A peaceful heart leads to a healthy body;
jealousy is like cancer in the bones.
Proverbs 14:30 NLT

Judging

God alone, who gave the law, is the Judge. He alone has the power to save or to destroy. So what right do you have to judge your neighbor?

James 4:12 NLT

Do you suppose, O man—you who judge those who practice such things and yet do them yourself—that you will escape the judgment of God?

Romans 2:3 ESV

Brothers and sisters, if someone is caught in a sin, you who live by the Spirit should restore that person gently. But watch yourselves, or you also may be tempted.

Galatians 6:1 NIV

"Do not judge according to appearance, but judge with righteous judgment."

John 7:24 NKJV

Justice

Blessed are those who act justly,
who always do what is right.
Psalm 106:3 NIV

"Learn to do good; seek justice,
rebuke the oppressor; defend the
fatherless, plead for the widow."
Isaiah 1:17 NKJV

"He has told you, O man, what is good;
and what does the LORD require of you
but to do justice, and to love kindness,
and to walk humbly with your God?"
Micah 6:8 ESV

The LORD loves righteousness and justice;
the earth is full of His unfailing love.
Psalm 33:5 NIV

Leadership

Obey your leaders and submit to them,
for they are keeping watch over your
souls, as those who will have to give
an account. Let them do this with
joy and not with groaning, for that
would be of no advantage to you.
Hebrews 13:17 ESV

You have heard me teach things that
have been confirmed by many reliable
witnesses. Now teach these truths to
other trustworthy people who will
be able to pass them on to others.
2 Timothy 2:2 NLT

"Whoever wants to be a leader
among you must be your servant."
Matthew 20:26 NLT

Limitations

"Mortals, born of woman,
are of few days and full of trouble."
Job 14:1 NIV

"Can you search out the deep
things of God? Can you find out
the limits of the Almighty?"
Job 11:7 NKJV

And the LORD said to Moses,
"Is the LORD's hand shortened?
Now you shall see whether My word
will come true for you or not."
Numbers 11:23 ESV

"For the one whom God has sent
speaks the words of God, for God
gives the Spirit without limit."
John 3:34 NIV

Listening

"Here I am! I stand at the door
and knock. If anyone hears My voice
and opens the door, I will come in and
eat with that person, and they with Me."
Revelation 3:20 NIV

"Call to Me, and I will answer you,
and show you great and mighty things,
which you do not know."
Jeremiah 33:3 NKJV

"Then you will call upon Me and go
and pray to Me, and I will listen to you."
Jeremiah 29:12 NKJV

I love the LORD because He hears
my voice and my prayer for mercy.
Because He bends down to listen,
I will pray as long as I have breath!
Psalm 116:1-2 NLT

Loneliness

Turn to me and be gracious to me,
for I am lonely and afflicted.
Psalm 25:16 ESV

Even if my father and mother abandon
me, the LORD will hold me close.
Psalm 27:10 NLT

Trust in Him at all times, you
people; pour out your heart before
Him; God is a refuge for us.
Psalm 62:8 NKJV

"Do not be afraid or discouraged, for
the LORD will personally go ahead
of you. He will be with you; He will
neither fail you nor abandon you."
Deuteronomy 31:8 NLT

Love

"A new commandment I give to you,
that you love one another;
as I have loved you, that you also
love one another. By this all will
know that you are My disciples,
if you have love for one another."
John 13:34-35 NKJV

"For the Father Himself loves you,
because you have loved Me and have
believed that I came from God."
John 16:27 ESV

Three things will last forever—faith, hope,
and love—and the greatest of these is love.
1 Corinthians 13:13 NLT

Whoever does not love does not
know God, because God is love.
1 John 4:8 NIV

Loyalty

Steadfast love and faithfulness
preserve the king, and by steadfast
love his throne is upheld.
Proverbs 20:28 ESV

Never let loyalty and kindness leave you!
Tie them around your neck as a reminder.
Write them deep within your heart.
Proverbs 3:3 NLT

But Ruth said, "Do not urge me to
leave you or to return from following you.
For where you go I will go, and where
you lodge I will lodge. Your people shall
be my people, and your God my God."
Ruth 1:16 ESV

A man of many companions may
come to ruin, but there is a friend
who sticks closer than a brother.
Proverbs 18:24 ESV

Lust

"But I tell you that anyone who looks at a woman lustfully has already committed adultery with her in his heart."
Matthew 5:28 NIV

Put to death therefore what is earthly in you: sexual immorality, impurity, passion, evil desire, and covetousness, which is idolatry.
Colossians 3:5 ESV

Temptation comes from our own desires, which entice us and drag us away. These desires give birth to sinful actions. And when sin is allowed to grow, it gives birth to death.
James 1:14-15 NLT

I say then: Walk in the Spirit, and you shall not fulfill the lust of the flesh.
Galatians 5:16 NKJV

Materialism

Those who love money will never have enough. How meaningless to think that wealth brings true happiness!
Ecclesiastes 5:10 NLT

"But all too quickly the message is crowded out by the worries of this life, the lure of wealth, and the desire for other things, so no fruit is produced."
Mark 4:19 NLT

"Sell what you have and give alms; provide yourselves money bags which do not grow old, a treasure in the heavens that does not fail, where no thief approaches nor moth destroys. For where your treasure is, there your heart will be also."
Luke 12:33-34 NKJV

Meekness

"Blessed are the meek,
for they shall inherit the earth."
Matthew 5:5 NKJV

Who is wise and understanding
among you? By his good conduct
let him show his works in
the meekness of wisdom.
James 3:13 ESV

Put on then, as God's chosen ones, holy
and beloved, compassionate hearts,
kindness, humility, meekness, and patience.
Colossians 3:12 ESV

But the meek will inherit the land
and enjoy peace and prosperity.
Psalm 37:11 NIV

Money

"No one can serve two masters,
for either he will hate the one
and love the other, or he will be devoted
to the one and despise the other.
You cannot serve God and money."
Matthew 6:24 ESV

Give me an eagerness for Your laws
rather than a love for money!
Psalm 119:36 NLT

Trust in your money and down you go!
But the godly flourish like leaves in spring.
Proverbs 11:28 NLT

"Why spend money on what is not bread,
and your labor on what does not satisfy?
Listen, listen to Me, and eat what is good,
and you will delight in the richest of fare."
Isaiah 55:2 NIV

Motives

The LORD's light penetrates
the human spirit,
exposing every hidden motive.
Proverbs 20:27 NLT

"For the LORD sees not as man sees:
man looks on the outward appearance,
but the LORD looks on the heart."
1 Samuel 16:7 ESV

Do not those who plot evil go astray?
But those who plan what is good
find love and faithfulness.
Proverbs 14:22 NIV

"Watch out! Don't do your good deeds
publicly, to be admired by others,
for you will lose the reward
from your Father in heaven."
Matthew 6:1 NLT

Obedience

In fact, this is love for God: to
keep His commands. And His
commands are not burdensome.
1 John 5:3 NIV

"You shall be careful to do as the LORD your
God has commanded you; you shall not
turn aside to the right hand or to the left."
Deuteronomy 5:32 NKJV

I have chosen the way of faithfulness;
I set Your rules before me.
Psalm 119:30 ESV

For just as through the disobedience of
the one man the many were made sinners,
so also through the obedience of the one
man the many will be made righteous.
Romans 5:19 NIV

Opportunities

Therefore, as we have opportunity,
let us do good to all, especially to those
who are of the household of faith.
Galatians 6:10 NKJV

Then He said to His disciples,
"The harvest is plentiful, but the
laborers are few; therefore pray earnestly
to the Lord of the harvest to send
out laborers into His harvest."
Matthew 9:37-38 ESV

"I know all the things you do,
and I have opened a door for you
that no one can close. You have
little strength, yet you obeyed My
word and did not deny Me."
Revelation 3:8 NLT

Opposition

Do not repay evil with evil or insult with insult. On the contrary, repay evil with blessing, because to this you were called so that you may inherit a blessing.

1 Peter 3:9 NIV

"Love your enemies, bless those who curse you, do good to those who hate you, and pray for those who spitefully use you and persecute you."

Matthew 5:44 NKJV

If you are suffering in a manner that pleases God, keep on doing what is right, and trust your lives to the God who created you, for He will never fail you.

1 Peter 4:19 NLT

Patience

A hot-tempered person stirs up conflict,
but the one who is patient calms a quarrel.
Proverbs 15:18 NIV

Better is the end of a thing than its
beginning, and the patient in spirit
is better than the proud in spirit.
Ecclesiastes 7:8 ESV

Love is patient, love is kind. It does not
envy, it does not boast, it is not proud.
1 Corinthians 13:4 NIV

Since God chose you to be the holy people
He loves, you must clothe yourselves
with tenderhearted mercy, kindness,
humility, gentleness, and patience.
Colossians 3:12 NLT

Persistence

Let us not grow weary while doing
good, for in due season we shall
reap if we do not lose heart.
Galatians 6:9 NKJV

"Ask and it will be given to you;
seek and you will find; knock and
the door will be opened to you.
For everyone who asks receives; the one
who seeks finds; and to the one who
knocks, the door will be opened."
Luke 11:9-10 NIV

Search for the Lord and for
His strength; continually seek Him.
1 Chronicles 16:11 NLT

Don't get sidetracked;
keep your feet from following evil.
Proverbs 4:27 NLT

Planning

A prudent man foresees evil
and hides himself, but the simple
pass on and are punished.
Proverbs 22:3 NKJV

Wise people think before they act;
fools don't—and even brag
about their foolishness.
Proverbs 13:16 NLT

Many are the plans in the mind
of a man, but it is the purpose
of the LORD that will stand.
Proverbs 19:21 ESV

Prepare your outside work,
make it fit for yourself in the field;
and afterward build your house.
Proverbs 24:27 NKJV

Pleasure

I said to myself, "Come on,
let's try pleasure. Let's look for the
'good things' in life." But I found
that this, too, was meaningless.
Ecclesiastes 2:1 NLT

Whoever loves pleasure will be a poor man;
he who loves wine and oil will not be rich.
Proverbs 21:17 ESV

You have put more joy in
my heart than they have when
their grain and wine abound.
Psalm 4:7 ESV

You will show me the way of life,
granting me the joy of Your presence
and the pleasures of living with You forever.
Psalm 16:11 NLT

Poor

"For there will never cease to be poor
in the land. Therefore I command you,
'You shall open wide your hand
to your brother, to the needy
and to the poor, in your land.'"

Deuteronomy 15:11 ESV

He who has pity on the poor
lends to the Lord, and He will
pay back what he has given.

Proverbs 19:17 NKJV

Whoever oppresses the poor shows
contempt for their Maker, but whoever
is kind to the needy honors God.

Proverbs 14:31 NIV

Those who shut their ears to
the cries of the poor will be
ignored in their own time of need.

Proverbs 21:13 NLT

Power

Not that we are sufficient of ourselves to
think of anything as being from ourselves,
but our sufficiency is from God.

2 Corinthians 3:5 NKJV

For God gave us a spirit not of fear
but of power and love and self-control.

2 Timothy 1:7 ESV

"But you will receive power when the
Holy Spirit comes on you; and you will be
My witnesses in Jerusalem, and in all Judea
and Samaria, and to the ends of the earth."

Acts 1:8 NIV

"The eyes of the LORD search the
whole earth in order to strengthen those
whose hearts are fully committed to Him."

2 Chronicles 16:9 NLT

Prayer

Do not be anxious about anything,
but in everything by prayer
and supplication with thanksgiving
let your requests be made known to God.
Philippians 4:6 ESV

Continue earnestly in prayer,
being vigilant in it with thanksgiving.
Colossians 4:2 NKJV

"Call to Me and I will answer you
and tell you great and unsearchable
things you do not know."
Jeremiah 33:3 NIV

Confess your trespasses to one another,
and pray for one another, that you may
be healed. The effective, fervent prayer
of a righteous man avails much.
James 5:16 NKJV

Pride

"Your heart was proud
because of your beauty."
Ezekiel 28:17 ESV

Pride goes before destruction,
and a haughty spirit before a fall.
Proverbs 16:18 NKJV

A man's pride will bring him low,
but the humble in spirit
will retain honor.
Proverbs 29:23 NKJV

But He gives us more grace.
That is why Scripture says:
"God opposes the proud
but shows favor to the humble."
James 4:6 NIV

Profanity

Let there be no filthiness nor foolish talk
nor crude joking, which are out of place,
but instead let there be thanksgiving.
Ephesians 5:4 ESV

But now you yourselves are to put off
all these: anger, wrath, malice, blasphemy,
filthy language out of your mouth.
Colossians 3:8 NKJV

"I tell you this, you must give
an account on judgment day for
every idle word you speak."
Matthew 12:36 NLT

From the same mouth come
blessing and cursing. My brothers,
these things ought not to be so.
James 3:10 ESV

Purpose

"For I know the plans I have for you,"
declares the LORD, "plans to prosper
you and not to harm you, plans to
give you hope and a future."
Jeremiah 29:11 NIV

The end of the matter; all has been heard.
Fear God and keep His commandments,
for this is the whole duty of man.
Ecclesiastes 12:13 ESV

For we are His workmanship, created
in Christ Jesus for good works,
which God prepared beforehand
that we should walk in them.
Ephesians 2:10 NKJV

The LORD has made everything
for His own purposes, even the
wicked for a day of disaster.
Proverbs 16:4 NLT

Reconciliation

But now in Christ Jesus you who
once were far off have been brought
near by the blood of Christ.
Ephesians 2:13 NKJV

Through Him God reconciled everything
to Himself. He made peace with
everything in heaven and on earth by
means of Christ's blood on the cross.
Colossians 1:20 NLT

…by canceling the record of debt that
stood against us with its legal demands.
This He set aside, nailing it to the cross.
Colossians 2:14 ESV

Therefore, since we have been justified
through faith, we have peace with
God through our Lord Jesus Christ.
Romans 5:1 NIV

Regrets

For I recognize my rebellion; it haunts
me day and night. Against You, and
You alone, have I sinned; I have
done what is evil in Your sight.
Psalm 51:3-4 NLT

"They will loathe themselves for
the evils which they committed in
all their abominations. And they
shall know that I am the LORD."
Ezekiel 6:9-10 NKJV

Godly sorrow brings repentance that
leads to salvation and leaves no regret,
but worldly sorrow brings death.
2 Corinthians 7:10 NIV

When Judas, who had betrayed Him,
realized that Jesus had been condemned
to die, he was filled with remorse.
Matthew 27:3 NLT

Repentance

"Repent, then, and turn to God,
so that your sins may be wiped
out, that times of refreshing
may come from the Lord."

Acts 3:19 NIV

He who covers his sins will
not prosper, but whoever confesses
and forsakes them will have mercy.

Proverbs 28:13 NKJV

Let the wicked forsake their ways
and the unrighteous their thoughts.
Let them turn to the LORD, and He
will have mercy on them, and to our
God, for He will freely pardon.

Isaiah 55:7 NIV

"Repent of your sins and turn to God,
for the Kingdom of Heaven is near."

Matthew 3:2 NLT

Reputation

"Take heed that you do not
do your charitable deeds
before men, to be seen by them."
Matthew 6:1 NKJV

For this very reason, make every effort
to supplement your faith with virtue.
2 Peter 1:5 ESV

Live such good lives among the pagans
that, though they accuse you of doing
wrong, they may see your good deeds
and glorify God on the day He visits us.
1 Peter 2:12 NIV

"Let your light so shine before men,
that they may see your good works
and glorify your Father in heaven."
Matthew 5:16 NKJV

Respect

"Stand up in the presence of the
elderly, and show respect for the aged.
Fear your God. I am the LORD."
Leviticus 19:32 NLT

Slaves, obey your earthly masters with respect
and fear, and with sincerity of heart, just
as you would obey Christ…And masters,
treat your slaves in the same way. Do not
threaten them, since you know that He who
is both their Master and yours is in heaven.
Ephesians 6:5, 9 NIV

Respect everyone, and love the family
of believers. Fear God, and respect the king.
1 Peter 2:17 NLT

"Therefore, whatever you want
men to do to you, do also to them,
for this is the Law and the Prophets."
Matthew 7:12 NKJV

Responsibility

For each one shall bear his own load.
Galatians 6:5 NKJV

He who plants and he who waters
are one, and each will receive his
wages according to his labor.
1 Corinthians 3:8 ESV

"All people will die for their own sins—
those who eat the sour grapes will be
the ones whose mouths will pucker."
Jeremiah 31:30 NLT

"He who is faithful in what is least is
faithful also in much; and he who is unjust
in what is least is unjust also in much."
Luke 16:10 NKJV

So then, each of us will give
an account of ourselves to God.
Romans 14:12 NIV

Rest

On the seventh day God had
finished His work of creation,
so He rested from all His work.
Genesis 2:2 NLT

"Come to Me, all you who
labor and are heavy laden,
and I will give you rest."
Matthew 11:28 NKJV

In peace I will lie down and sleep,
for You alone, Lord,
make me dwell in safety.
Psalm 4:8 NLT

He said to them, "Come aside by
yourselves to a deserted place
and rest a while." For there were
many coming and going, and they
did not even have time to eat.
Mark 6:31 NKJV

Revival

"Now repent of your sins and turn to God,
so that your sins may be wiped away.
Then times of refreshment will come from
the presence of the Lord, and He will again
send you Jesus, your appointed Messiah."
Acts 3:19-20 NLT

"And I will give you a new heart,
and a new spirit I will put within you.
And I will remove the heart of stone from
your flesh and give you a heart of flesh."
Ezekiel 36:26 ESV

"Sow for yourselves righteousness;
reap in mercy; break up your fallow ground,
for it is time to seek the LORD, till He
comes and rains righteousness on you."
Hosea 10:12 NKJV

Salvation

"For God so loved the world that
He gave His only begotten Son,
that whoever believes in Him should
not perish but have everlasting life."
John 3:16 NKJV

If you confess with your mouth
that Jesus is Lord and believe in
your heart that God raised Him
from the dead, you will be saved.
Romans 10:9 ESV

Jesus answered, "I am the way
and the truth and the life. No one
comes to the Father except through Me."
John 14:6 NIV

For the wages of sin is death,
but the free gift of God is eternal life
through Christ Jesus our Lord.
Romans 6:23 NLT

Seduction

And now, O sons, listen to me,
and do not depart from the words of
my mouth. Keep your way far from her,
and do not go near the door of her house.
Proverbs 5:7-8 ESV

Above all else, guard your heart,
for everything you do flows from it.
Proverbs 4:23 NIV

And I find more bitter than death
the woman whose heart is snares
and nets, whose hands are fetters.
He who pleases God shall escape from her,
but the sinner shall be trapped by her.
Ecclesiastes 7:26 NKJV

Don't lust for her beauty.
Don't let her coy glances seduce you.
Proverbs 6:25 NLT

Self-Control

But I discipline my body
and bring it into subjection, lest,
when I have preached to others,
I myself should become disqualified.
1 Corinthians 9:27 NKJV

He must be hospitable, one who loves
what is good, who is self-controlled,
upright, holy and disciplined.
Titus 1:8 NIV

Take control of what I say,
O Lord, and guard my lips.
Psalm 141:3 NLT

Older men are to be sober-minded,
dignified, self-controlled, sound in
faith, in love, and in steadfastness.
Titus 2:2 ESV

Sensitivity

We who are strong must be considerate
of those who are sensitive about things
like this. We must not just please ourselves.
Romans 15:1 NLT

"If among you, one of your brothers
should become poor, in any of
your towns within your land that the
LORD your God is giving you, you shall
not harden your heart or shut your
hand against your poor brother."
Deuteronomy 15:7 ESV

"The Spirit of the Sovereign LORD is
on me, because the LORD has anointed me
to proclaim good news to the poor.
He has sent me to bind up the brokenhearted,
to proclaim freedom for the captives
and release from darkness for the prisoners."
Isaiah 61:1 NIV

Sin

Wash away all my iniquity and cleanse me
from my sin. For I know my transgressions,
and my sin is always before me.

Psalm 51:2-3 NIV

Surely there is not a righteous man
on earth who does good and never sins.

Ecclesiastes 7:20 ESV

If we say that we have no sin, we deceive
ourselves, and the truth is not in us.
If we confess our sins, He is faithful
and just to forgive us our sins and to
cleanse us from all unrighteousness.

1 John 1:8-9 NKJV

Submit yourselves, then, to God.
Resist the devil, and he will flee from you.

James 4:7 NIV

Stress

Out of my distress I called on the LORD;
the LORD answered me and set me free.
The LORD is on my side; I will not fear.
What can man do to me?
Psalm 118:5-6 ESV

Blessed is the man who endures temptation;
for when he has been approved, he will
receive the crown of life which the Lord
has promised to those who love Him.
James 1:12 NKJV

When anxiety was great within me,
Your consolation brought me joy.
Psalm 94:19 NIV

I know the LORD is always with me.
I will not be shaken,
for He is right beside me.
Psalm 16:8 NLT

Success

Commit your work to the Lord,
and your plans will be established.
Proverbs 16:3 ESV

For I can do everything through
Christ, who gives me strength.
Philippians 4:13 NLT

Honor the Lord with your wealth,
with the firstfruits of all your crops;
then your barns will be filled to
overflowing, and your vats will
brim over with new wine.
Proverbs 3:9-10 NIV

"Remember the Lord your God.
He is the one who gives
you power to be successful."
Deuteronomy 8:18 NLT

Teamwork

Behold, how good and how pleasant it is
for brethren to dwell together in unity!
Psalm 133:1 NKJV

I appeal to you, brothers, by the name
of our Lord Jesus Christ, that all of
you agree, and that there be no divisions
among you, but that you be united in
the same mind and the same judgment.
1 Corinthians 1:10 ESV

May the God who gives endurance
and encouragement give you the same
attitude of mind toward each other that
Christ Jesus had, so that with one mind
and one voice you may glorify the God
and Father of our Lord Jesus Christ.
Romans 15:5-6 NIV

Temptation

No temptation has overtaken you except what is common to mankind. And God is faithful; He will not let you be tempted beyond what you can bear. But when you are tempted, He will also provide a way out so that you can endure it.

1 Corinthians 10:13 NIV

"And lead us not into temptation, but deliver us from evil."

Matthew 6:13 ESV

So humble yourselves before God. Resist the devil, and he will flee from you.

James 4:7 NLT

Let no one say when he is tempted, "I am tempted by God"; for God cannot be tempted by evil, nor does He Himself tempt anyone.

James 1:13 NKJV

Thoughts

For those who live according to
the flesh set their minds on the things
of the flesh, but those who live according
to the Spirit, the things of the Spirit.
For to be carnally minded is death, but to
be spiritually minded is life and peace.

Romans 8:5-6 NKJV

Finally, brothers, whatever is true,
whatever is honorable, whatever is just,
whatever is pure, whatever is lovely,
whatever is commendable, if there is any
excellence, if there is anything worthy
of praise, think about these things.

Philippians 4:8 ESV

"You will keep in perfect peace
all who trust in You, all whose
thoughts are fixed on You!"

Isaiah 26:3 NLT

Tithing

"Bring the full tithe into the storehouse,
that there may be food in My house.
And thereby put Me to the test,
says the LORD of hosts, if I will not
open the windows of heaven for you
and pour down for you a blessing
until there is no more need."

Malachi 3:10 ESV

"Will man rob God? Yet you are robbing Me.
But you say, 'How have we robbed You?'
In your tithes and contributions."

Malachi 3:8 ESV

"I have shown you in every way,
by laboring like this, that you must
support the weak. And remember the
words of the Lord Jesus, that He said,
'It is more blessed to give than to receive.'"

Acts 20:35 NKJV

Truth

"For God is Spirit, so those who worship
Him must worship in spirit and in truth."
John 4:24 NLT

Lead me in Your truth and teach me,
for You are the God of my salvation;
for You I wait all the day long.
Psalm 25:5 ESV

"When He, the Spirit of truth, has come,
He will guide you into all truth; for He
will not speak on His own authority,
but whatever He hears He will speak;
and He will tell you things to come."
John 16:13 NKJV

Do your best to present yourself to
God as one approved, a worker who
does not need to be ashamed and who
correctly handles the word of truth.
2 Timothy 2:15 NIV

Vision

Then the LORD answered me and said:
"Write the vision and make it plain on
tablets, that he may run who reads it."
Habakkuk 2:2 NKJV

Because I am righteous, I will see You.
When I awake, I will see You
face to face and be satisfied.
Psalm 17:15 NLT

"I will pour out my Spirit on all people.
Your sons and daughters will prophesy,
your old men will dream dreams,
your young men will see visions."
Joel 2:28 NIV

Those who look to Him are radiant,
and their faces shall never be ashamed.
Psalm 34:5 ESV

Vulnerability

Search me, God, and know my heart;
test me and know my anxious thoughts.
See if there is any offensive way in me,
and lead me in the way everlasting.
Psalm 139:23-24 NIV

Sometimes you were exposed to
public ridicule and were beaten,
and sometimes you helped others who
were suffering the same things.
Hebrews 10:33 NLT

"Blessed are you when people insult you,
persecute you and falsely say all kinds of
evil against you because of Me. Rejoice and
be glad, because great is your reward in
heaven, for in the same way they persecuted
the prophets who were before you."
Matthew 5:11-12 NIV

Wisdom

If any of you lacks wisdom, let him ask
God, who gives generously to all without
reproach, and it will be given him.
James 1:5 ESV

For the Lord gives wisdom;
from His mouth come knowledge
and understanding.
Proverbs 2:6 NKJV

But the wisdom that comes from heaven
is first of all pure; then peace-loving,
considerate, submissive, full of mercy
and good fruit, impartial and sincere.
James 3:17 NIV

Getting wisdom is the wisest thing
you can do! And whatever else you
do, develop good judgment.
Proverbs 4:7 NLT

Witnessing

Has the LORD redeemed you?
Then speak out! Tell others He has
redeemed you from your enemies.
Psalm 107:2 NLT

And He said to them,
"Go into all the world and preach
the gospel to every creature."
Mark 16:15 NKJV

Jesus said to them, "Follow Me,
and I will make you
become fishers of men."
Mark 1:17 NKJV

Rescue others by snatching them from the
flames of judgment. Show mercy to still
others, but do so with great caution, hating
the sins that contaminate their lives.
Jude 1:23 NLT

Wives

Your wife will be like a fruitful vine
within your house; your children
will be like olive shoots around
your table. Behold, thus shall the
man be blessed who fears the LORD.
Psalm 128:3-4 ESV

He who finds a wife finds a good thing,
and obtains favor from the LORD.
Proverbs 18:22 NKJV

Husbands, love your wives
and never treat them harshly.
Colossians 3:19 NLT

Likewise, husbands, live with your wives
in an understanding way, showing honor
to the woman as the weaker vessel, since
they are heirs with you of the grace of life,
so that your prayers may not be hindered.
1 Peter 3:7 ESV

Word of God

For the word of God is living
and active, sharper than any
two-edged sword, piercing to the
division of soul and of spirit, of joints
and of marrow, and discerning the
thoughts and intentions of the heart.
Hebrews 4:12 ESV

Your word is a lamp to my feet
and a light to my path.
Psalm 119:105 NKJV

Your word, LORD, is eternal;
it stands firm in the heavens.
Psalm 119:89 NIV

They have made God's law their own,
so they will never slip from His path.
Psalm 37:31 NLT

Words

Don't use foul or abusive language.
Let everything you say be good
and helpful, so that your words will be
an encouragement to those who hear them.
Ephesians 4:29 NLT

Death and life are in the power
of the tongue, and those who
love it will eat its fruit.
Proverbs 18:21 NKJV

Do you see a man who is hasty
in his words? There is more hope
for a fool than for him.
Proverbs 29:20 ESV

Gracious words are a honeycomb,
sweet to the soul and healing to the bones.
Proverbs 16:24 NIV

Work

Let the favor of the Lord our God
be upon us, and establish the
work of our hands upon us; yes,
establish the work of our hands!
Psalm 90:17 ESV

And whatever you do or say, do it as a
representative of the Lord Jesus, giving
thanks through Him to God the Father.
Colossians 3:17 NLT

Whatever you do, work heartily,
as for the Lord and not for men.
Colossians 3:23 ESV

Then the LORD God took
the man and put him in the
garden of Eden to tend and keep it.
Genesis 2:15 NKJV

Worry

"You will be secure, because there
is hope; you will look about you
and take your rest in safety."
Job 11:18 NIV

Cast your burden on the LORD,
and He will sustain you; He will never
permit the righteous to be moved.
Psalm 55:22 ESV

"So do not fear, for I am with you;
do not be dismayed, for I am your God.
I will strengthen you and help you; I will
uphold you with my righteous right hand."
Isaiah 41:10 NIV

"Do not worry about tomorrow,
for tomorrow will worry about
its own things. Sufficient for
the day is its own trouble."
Matthew 6:34 NKJV

Worship

Give to the LORD the glory
He deserves! Bring your offering
and come into His presence.
Worship the LORD in all His holy splendor.

1 Chronicles 16:29 NLT

It is good to praise the LORD and make
music to Your name, O Most High,
proclaiming Your love in the morning
and Your faithfulness at night.

Psalm 92:1-2 NIV

I will extol You, my God and King,
and bless Your name forever and ever.
Every day I will bless You
and praise Your name forever and ever.

Psalm 145:1-2 ESV

I will be glad and rejoice in You; I will
sing praise to Your name, O Most High.

Psalm 9:2 NKJV